More than 1,000
women were asked one Bold Question

Live Better Dads
Live Better Daughters

11 Power Principles,
Conscious Dads,
Real Results

Also, in Audio Format

BY: LONDON PORTER

Twitter @LondonPorter
www.LondonPorter.Co
www.iblb23.com

DEDICATION

To My Angels on Earth and Beyond:

Cali Juliana Porter
Julia Porter
Helen Porter-Ferguson
Alice Whetts

Table of Contents

Introduction:

This book is possible because I asked 1,000 women One Bold Question.

"What are 3 or 4 things a dad must do, be, or say to raise a confident, successful daughter in today's society?"

I condensed all the responses into 11 power principles.

But first, some real talk. With respect to you and your daughter this book is:

- A tool for you
- A tool to start more conversations
- A tool to question what you've been taught
- An invitation to effectively analyze what results you are current getting
- An invitation to create or refine your Live Better Dad blueprint
- An invitation to help your daughter **fall even deeper in love with you** and your actions

With respect to you and your daughter, this book is *not*:

- Anything you don't want it to be. Period.

This book is the first of three and it will be published February 14, 2017. If, at the end, you find value in the conversation we're about to have, connect with me on LinkedIn or twitter.

@londonporter

If you have an idea, a story, or an insight for a chapter in the next book, reach out to me. This is formal invitation to you.

Next, this book is set up to maximize your time. Each chapter follows a simple format:

1. The Wisdom, which is a quote
2. The Event, a conversation between my daughter, Cali, and me
3. The Action item, a task or action you may want to consider doing
4. The Take Away, is the lesson learned;
5. The Resource, a way to learn more on your own Straight Whiskey - No Chaser, a candid, unedited talk from me to you. And...the straight whiskey section is only available in audio book format.

Again, The Wisdom, The Event, The Action Item, The Take Away, The Resource, and Straight Whiskey - No Chaser.

Twitter @LondonPorter
www.LondonPorter.Co
www.iblb23.com

Chapter 1

Be Here
and Now for Her

The Wisdom:

"Trust is gained in drops and lost in buckets."
Author: Unknown

The Event:

"Dad, want to play with me?"
"Not now, babe, I'm working on something."
"Well, let me show you the horse stable I created
real quick…"

"Okay, real quick."
"Here's the entrance, when you walk in…"
Instead of paying attention, I was working on my
laptop.
"Forget it, you're not looking."
"You know, hon, you're right. Dad wasn't looking. I
apologize. But guess what?"
"What?"
"Gimmie that controller. I am making 20 minutes
just for you and me. Zero interruptions, deal?"
"Deal."

"And then zero interruptions when Dad's doing his
work…deal?"
"Deal."
"Now show me how build a feeding trough for
these horses in your stable."
"But you're not good at Minecraft, that'll take too
long."

"Well, let's see how far we can get in 20 minutes. What's this button do?"

The Action Item:

I consider myself an ambitious fellow. A man in love with passion, dreams, and I value action over talk. What dreams do you have? What physical items must you possess to consider yourself successful? How much money will you make this month? This ambition and these dreams of yours and mine can easily blind us and lie to us.

Our dreams whisper in our ear and say, "You're doing this for her, for her future, her education, her car, her independence, her success…"

Me, I am not an advice giver. I am a resource provider. Use the continuous re-calibration tools in your heart and mind to determine when your dreams require your attention and when your daughter requires it more. Decide that you will:

- Be better at creating uninterrupted time for your daughter
- Get down to eye level with your daughter when she's telling you something important to her
- Set up a pattern or frequency to take your daughter out on dates
- Forgive yourself when you know your actions fail to give her your undivided

- attention she silent asks for, she deserves, and she craves.
- If you're bold enough, allow her to be your accountability partner and give her permission to take you to task and unapologetically blow the whistle when your lack of attention goes out of bounds.

The Take Away:

When you are aware of, when you work on, and when you master the art of creating more moments of giving your daughter your exclusive and total attention:

- You deepen the trust she has in you
- You show her how a man she loves should pay attention to her
- You produce a habit, an attractive quality in yourself, that serves you well in both your personal and professional life

The Resource:

Ted Talk by Matt Killingsworth: Stay in the Moment.

The Straight Whiskey, No Chaser:

This was an absolute hot button during the survey. More than 80% of 1,000 women said that fathers need to pay attention more…100% full on attention and really listen.

Here's why. It's a must because it builds trust.

To seed and grow this trust and you have to show up hyper focused, without an agenda to solve a problem, and to be nonjudgmental without interruptions.

These are some of the qualities in full on listening. Hey, I will be the first to raise my hand, as I mentioned previously, I did not live up to this expectation in the past and I had to learn too.

If your daughter is shorter than you, get on her eye level. Look her eye to eye. If she's taller than you, jump on a stool and get on her eye level.

Put down the phone, put down the laptop, put down the hologram if it's 20 years from now and pay attention. Speak it out loud, "Babe, I'm removing all these distractions. You have my full undivided attention. What do you need, sweetie?"

When you cultivate this habit in yourself, here's something interesting that happens. At work, at the bank, at the restaurant, people treat you differently.

Try this the next time you go out to eat. The waiter or waitress arrives and you say, "Hey, what's your name?"
"Ralph."
"Hey Ralph, thanks for serving us tonight."
Then see what type of service that you get. When you cultivate this habit of being in the moment,

weave it into your communication fabric of life, you will find that people connect with you on a completely different level.

Don't believe me. Try it for yourself, see how it goes, and report back to me on Twitter @londonporter.

"Trust is gained in drops and lost in buckets."

Author: Unknown

Chapter 2

Be Her Training Ground For Life

The Wisdom:

"For there is nothing either good or bad, thinking makes it so." ~Shakespeare

The Event:

She ran down the stairs so fast, her momentum almost plowed me over before I dodged her in the kitchen.
"Dad, Mya's outside...can I go play?"

"Is your room clean?"
"Uh, yeah."
"Is your room clean, baby?"
"No."
"Why'd you lie to me like that?"

That was my response the first time this happened. How do you think it made Cali feel? How do you think I felt? After doing a lot of work developing my personal philosophy of being a better person, man, and dad...this is how the conversation went the next time.

"Dad, the dog's outside...can I go play?"
"Is your room clean?"
"Yeah."
"Cal, is your room clean?"
"No."

"Nice try, babe, I almost believed you. Quick, go

clean your room. The dogs are waiting…Go, go, go."

The Action Item:

No, I am not an advocate of lying. I am her self-esteem advocate, her mental health advocate, and her emotional intelligence advocate. Lying is a part of life. Would you agree? Examine your emotions around lying. Consider creating a thinking and response strategy.

Decide what you believe to be a

- minor lie
- medium lie
- a major lie
- or if all lies are the same

Decide if you are going to be a moral hypocrite or her father, who she can trust.

When I shared this topic at a conference, many men and women took offense to this mental strategy and said, "You should never lie." I asked every person who responded that way if they told a lie of any nature in the last three months. Not one person could say they did not lie in the last three months.

This is life. Be real. Get real. Develop real strategies.

Decide if the age of your daughter factors into how you respond to her lying. Cali was nine in this example.

Decide if the intent behind the lie factors into how you feel and think about a particular lie. For example, Cali lied because she was in the moment and momentum of fun. The genesis of her intention was not to deceive me. Her main desire was to play. Cali's intent played a factor with how I thought about the gravity of her lie. And you saw the difference of how I responded the first and second time. Decide if intent is a factor with you.

Does this concept resonate with you? Did it help guide you to a better concept? Is thinking about how you would respond in future situations worth your time? Is her future happiness worth your time? What she says about you when you're not around…is that worth your time?

Write down your thoughts in a notebook, your calendar, or any place you can review them later. Remember, thoughts that are transferred from inside your head to where your eyes can see them have power.

The Take Away:

You are her father, her first love, a place where she naturally expects to feel safe.

When a young woman feels safe, it's easier for her

to trust you, share with you, feel vulnerable with you, tell you her secrets, share her concerns, and reveal her dreams.

My reply the first time Cali lied about going outside did not make her feel safe. The next time it happened, I did create a safe space for her. A few days after the second instance, I spoke with Cali. Together, we discovered tips to help her be more influential when she really, really, really wants to do something instead of not telling me the truth.

And here's the experience-based secret you'll discover for yourself: Developing your personal philosophy for how you will deal with situations like lying will only strengthen your connection with her.

The Resource:
Why Women Lie Differently Than Men

http://www.huffingtonpost.com/susan-shapiro-barash/why-women-lie-differently_b_3007452.html

The Straight Whiskey, No Chaser:

This concept may be challenging if you have an extreme personality. I'll keep it simple. If you're all the way to the left of alpha male-ism or if you're all the way to the right of hyper-sensitivity-ism this idea may stretch you.

The alpha male is quick to fight, activate anger, and naturally uses forceful elements as a form of control.

When men lean too much into the sensitive side, they're focused on disappointment and hurt and they may use those emotions as manipulative elements of control to draw people in, especially their daughter.

What makes this so difficult is you must revisit the paradigms of what you've been taught, your religion, and your belief of what you consider respect.

What do you consider lying? What do you consider disrespect? What do you consider unfortunate realities that occur in life?

It takes a strong personality and a significant amount of courage to consider these internal questions.

Do you care more about defending your emotions, ego, and your learned morals more than growing your daughter's self-esteem, her emotional intelligence, her confidence, her critical thinking skills, her being able to utilize you as an interpersonal-skills playground, or your ability to be her safety net?

Or are you going to take out the whip and verbally, emotionally, or psychologically crack it on her when she's just expressing the art of being human, the art of being a growing young woman, the art of using the repertoire, the tools, everything that's inside of her that she can in a safe zone that's supposed to be created by you?

It's challenging, fellas. I am not going to lie or mince words here. However, based on the fact that you're reading this, I believe you are up to the challenge. And I believe you know she is worth it.

Chapter 3

En-Courage Her Curiosity

The Wisdom:

"Curiosity is the spark behind the spark of every great idea."
Author: Unknown

The Event:

"Why don't you love Mom anymore?"
"That's rude, Cali. Don't ask Dad questions like that."
"London, are you Cali's dad?"
"No."
"She can ask me anything. You can ask me anything. Am I clear?"
"Ummm hmmm."
"AM I CLEAR?"
"Yes, sir."
"Cal, you can ask me anything, anytime, anywhere."
"Thanks, Dad."
"Now, about your beautiful, gorgeous mom…"

The Action Item:

- How will you support her curiosity in life?
- Protect her from all threats, foreign and domestic?
- How well will you swallow your own uncomfortable thoughts around highly emotional topics?

- How will you create a safe space for her to challenge and question your actions?

Cali thought I didn't love Julia, her mom, my former first lady, because we didn't live in the same house. Location of domain overrode Cali's memories of all the other kind things I've said and done for Julia that Cali remembered. And that's not right or wrong of Cali, it was something she was curious about. And when Cali wants to know, she'll ask.

Decide that you will give a small amount of time to consider how, in your recent past, you have responded to personal questions that caught you off guard.

On a scale of 1 to 10, 10 being excellent and 1 being terrible, how would you rate the way you responded any kind of uncomfortable questions in general?

I rated myself 5 many years ago. Today, I'm a strong 8 and getting better day by day, year by year. And getting better takes work.

The Take Away:

When you were growing up, did you have a consistent adult male role model to have conversations like this with? I didn't. Maybe that's why you're reading, listening, or someone is sharing this experience with you now.

It lights up my soul's soul to see children smile...especially the forever child in me. The forever child in you. And the impact you can, will, and continue to have on her...your daughter.

Decide today that you will 'take away' one idea we have discovered together, sitting around this camp fire of words, you...and me. Write down the notes in your mind or on something near you.

Do it now. Your thoughts, your insights, and your power expressed from your mind through the pen is needed by your daughter, my daughter, and the other daughters who may not have men like you or me in their lives.

Take away a new tool to use, to share, and to inspire great actions in others.

The Resource:

Ted Talk: How to Retire by 20, Kristen Hadeed

In a hurry? Listen or watch minute 8:10 – 9:20 to see the impact curiosity has on daughters.

The Straight Whiskey, No Chaser:

When the data came back from the survey two things were very clear and evident. Number one, a lot of women said if you want to show your daughter how to be treated, always talk good about her mom whether you're together or not.

Always treat her mom with the utmost respect even when her mom's actions are not respectable.

Number two, was the quintessential thought of wishing their dads would have listened more, listened to how they felt, listened to the emotion behind the words, and not try to fix her or the problem (like we tend to do).

One of the respondents wrote the phrase 'deep listening'. She phrased it in such a way that prompted me to reach out to her. I wanted to know more. We were going back and forth on instant messenger and she said a dad should really listen to his daughter at any age and listen to her deeply.

Listen to how she feels and listen to where that feeling comes from. It would help if he learned to be comfortable being uncomfortable, he should hold a space of love for her, and help her figure out those answers herself by asking reflective questions?

She said that's what listening is all about, effective, deep listening, and listening at the seat of the soul if you will. **She said it would help men to understand how to ask smart questions when they feel uncomfortable.**

Again, she said it would help if men learned to ask

smart questions. If the hair didn't stand up on the back of your neck because of the truth that woman just shared with us I suggest you read that sentence again.

That's why this chapter is called "En-courage Her Curiosity." We are really simple creatures compared to women. We're innately one-track minded, we need a plan, we need a purpose, we thrive in the concept A to B, and we need a target to hit.

The more meaningful target should be how to en-courage her curiosity and the method that we use is deep listening coupled with asking smart questions…inside moments of feeling nervous, anxious, and uncomfortable when speaking with our daughters.

Our main goal is to en-courage our daughter to stand up for herself, have confidence, and have courage. In order for that to happen, we too, must exhibit vulnerable courage.

She's going to ask you questions that are going to flip your wig (shock you), and you got to stand strong in the face of that emotional storm.

You've got to be resilient, compassionate, and deliver in moments that cause your hands to start shaking as you hold them behind your back…and you look your daughter in the eye, stand in courage, and ask a question that inspires her to be en-couraged to share what's in her heart…with you.

Chapter 4

Lasso Your FFEE's

The Wisdom:

"You have two choices, control your mind or let it control you." ~Paulo Coelho

The Event:

"You don't look happy, Dad."
"Right now, I'm not, but you know what? Give Dad 7 minutes and I'll be better."
"Why 7 minutes?"
"That's how long I'll be exercising in the garage."
"Can I come?"
"Of course you can."

The Action Item:
True or False: Your daughter can do or say some things that take your breath away and she can do or say some things that make you want to take her breath away.

In the event above, Cali took my breath away when she showed me that I was bringing negative and foul attitudes into our home from work. And that she noticed and cared about how I felt.
FFEE's stands for Fear, Frustration, Ego, and Embarrassment.

I know a wildly successful children's author who hates children. I met a conflict resolution teacher who couldn't take a joke without turning red in the face with anger until she looked like a Washington apple. I used to be the dad who would occasionally bark orders at my daughter over silly things when I got home because I was tired, hungry, or emotionally worn out.

All forms of fear, frustration, ego, and embarrassment have at least one toe in the waters of stress and anxiety. Therefore, do you think it would make sense to develop your own stress and anxiety management system to decrease, not remove completely, but to decrease, the amount of, or length of time, of FFEE's in your life?

When I became disgusted at my behavior of barking orders at my daughter, a mentor helped me do some self-reflection.

- What time of the day did I typically act this way?
- Where was I going or coming from?
- What was on my mind prior to acting this way?
- Are there any similarities to what I was barking about?
- How serious or meaningful were the things I was ordering her to do?

Asking those questions helped me realize this nasty behavior of mine shined through when I got home from a challenging day at work, I noticed what she didn't do vs. what she did do when I opened the door. I typically had little patience, I was hungry, and my mind was still frustrated from the challenges I just left that were still spiraling in my head.

From there, my mentor and my mastermind group helped me create a simple game plan moving forward.

1. Apologize to Cali
2. Forgive myself
3. Take corrective action
4. Make Cali my accountability partner

The end result? I keep emergency protein bars in the car. When I'm having days when I allow work to emotionally tax my mind and energy, before I get home, I park around the corner, take off my shoes and socks, play a 3:31 second song I love, chew on a piece of my protein bar, wiggle my toes, breathe, smile, and unwind. And that's all it took to banish my silly behavior.

Keep in mind, what works for me may not work for you. The key is to find what does, do it, and measure your progress.

After walking into the house with a suit and flip-flops on, Cali figured out what was going on and after two weeks, she said I was more fun. That's all the accountability I needed.

Decide that you will watch your FFEEs like a hawk. And decide what you will do to quiet the negative emotions faster than they would dissolve if you didn't actively focus on them moving through you quickly.

The Take Away:

It's your choice. You can be as incongruent as a:

- Kleptomaniac Catholic
- Pro-life Abortion Physician
- Stress Free Trial Attorney

Or you can reach, stretch, learn, research, find, and continually discover ways to master the art of your FFEEs. If you won't do it for yourself, do it for her.

The Resource:

Book: *The Awakened Family* by Dr. Shefali Tsabary

The Straight Whiskey, No Chaser:

I was conducting a job interview recently, the candidate was a guy, and I asked him a question…something like, "Tell me about a time you made a big mistake at work that affected your coworkers. What happened and what did you do?"

The guy sat there in silence for a couple of seconds. "You know, I really can't think of something that has happened where I made a big mistake. I really try hard not to make big mistakes."

I was silent momentarily and looked him cautiously in the eye to give him one more chance. I said, "In the last year I can think of three mistakes I made. You're telling me in the last ten years you can't even think of one?"

He was silent again, "No, I really can't."

In my mind I was thinking, "Either you're not being honest or you are so unaware of your actions and how they affect the people around that you don't need to be at this organization." He did not get the job.

Guys, do you see how not working on your fees can cause you to lose opportunities, opportunities in your career, opportunities in your health, or opportunities with your daughter?

Before you try to make improvements in her behavior, make improvements in yours first.

Ending on a humorous note and in the words of Jim Rohn, "Work harder on yourself than you do on your job," than you do on your job of being her father, her dad, and her inspiration.

"You have two choices, control your mind or let it control you."

Author: Paulo Coelho

Chapter 5

What Role Will Sex and Sexuality Play in Her Life?

The Wisdom:

"Learn to be comfortable being uncomfortable."
Author: *Unknown*

The Event:

"Dad, what's the white stuff in your underwear?"
"Huh, what do you mean, Cal?"
"The white stuff in your underwear, what does that mean?"

It took a couple seconds, then I realized what my daughter was asking me. She was 11 years old at the time, going on 27, and her body was giving her hints that her menstrual cycle was near.

"Cal, that white stuff is called discharge and it's a great thing."
"Why is that?"
"It's how your body cleans itself…And…it's your body's way of talking to you."
"What's it saying?"
"It's tapping you on the shoulder and letting you know you will be starting your menstrual cycle soon."
"You mean my period?"
"Yeah, your period. Some women call it that, or menstrual cycle, moon cycle…?"
"I like moon cycle."
"Why is that?"

"I dunno, I just like it."

"Tell you what, let's bring Mom in on this, we can look at some pictures, and answer any questions you have about your moon cycle…how's that sound?"

"When?"

"Is tomorrow okay?"

"Sure."

The Action Item:

Decide that you will be the man to talk about any and all changes your daughter's body will go through. OR…let the kids at the playground educate her. How bad could that be, right? Potentially ignorant adolescents, the school nurse, or religious influences with heavily slanted views and guilt around sexuality.

- In 2015, over 64,000 teens got plastic surgery.
  Source: PlasticSurgery.org

Why do you think so many young women chose to undergo plastic surgery? How many more young women do you think would have said yes to 'the knife' if they had the money, the resources, or the wherewithal to do so? It's all to easy to blame the media, magazine covers, perfect figure play dolls, bullies, and the mean girls at school.

However, what is the mindset of my daughter, your

daughter, our daughters before they encounter any of those external influences?

Again, I don't claim to have the answers or solutions to complex body shaming and body image issues, however, I do believe that keeping the channels of real, raw, and uncomfortable communication open is certainly a positive vs a negative.

When Cali and I had that conversation, I kept as neutral an expression on my face as I could. Yes, the shock of emotion was raging on my alpha male insides. I remember thinking these two thoughts:

1. Don't try and fix it.
2. Keep it simple and speak in pictures.

The Take Away:

Decide that you will educate yourself as a man, a father, and a curious student of the human body about a woman's moon cycle. One of the main reasons your daughter may feel uncomfortable coming to you for advice or questions about sex and sexuality is because of the environment you've allowed her to be in and the one you have created. Naturally, her body looks different than yours and she may feel more comfortable speaking with a woman; however, that is zero excuse for your lack of knowledge, my lack of knowledge, about the specifics of how our daughter's bodies change over time.

When you have the knowledge, you are able to be a resource for your daughter. For example, if she's having a day of heavy cramping, your knowledge about her body and the subject will be able to offer suggestions to:

- decrease the intensity of her contracting muscles
- decrease stomach bloating
- decrease the heavy blood flow
- decrease the alone feeling
- increase the bond between you as a Live Better Dad and her as Live Better Daughter

The Resource:

Book: *Women's Bodies, Women's Wisdom: Creating Physical and Emotional Health and Healing,* by Christiane Northrup, M.D.

Internet Post/Article:
http://www.everydayhealth.com/treatment/women s-health/ways-to-relieve-period-cramps/

The Straight Whiskey, No Chaser:

Would it be safe to say this is an emotionally confrontational and provocative chapter?

You have a choice. You can have your daughter go through sex education, sex demonstration, or sex participation. Which one would you prefer? I thought so. I can hear you all the way over here screaming out, "Educationnnnnnn!"

There was one particular woman in the survey who was extraordinarily wise when it came to talking to young girls about sex. She said it very simply, "London, I speak about sex age appropriately."

"Whoa, whoa, whoa. Tell me more about that." She said, "Sure. If a five-year-old asks me where babies come from, I just say they come from the woman's belly."

Then she said if it's a ten-year-old in today's society, she would tell them the man and the woman come together, connect their bodies, and exchange the ingredients that cause a baby to begin to grow in the women's belly.

And if a 15 year old asked what does sex feel like, she was honest and brief, "Sometimes it can feel uncomfortable. Sometimes it feels exciting like the goose bumps on your skin and the chills that you get that tickle their way up the back of your spine."

The main point she expressed to me was she speaks age appropriately. The beauty was she said that a young girl or a child has never asked questions beyond their maturity level. But here's the catch. She said you must speak the truth. Be clear, be brief, and be genuine.

Speaking about being genuine, here's another tool you can use to find out more about your daughter's sensual and sexual proclivity and appetite for the subject.

It's numerology. Not astrology, even though there are astrological elements that coincide with numerology. However, let's focus strictly on the science of numbers.

There are many reputable and accurate online numerology programs out there. I'm not going to name them here. If you are interested to learn more, contact me on twitter:

@londonporter,

or just ask your circle of influence, meaning the individuals around you about reputable, in depth, and easy to use online numerology programs and numerology teachers. The benefit to you:

- Understanding the natural tendencies your daughter may have surrounding the dynamic issue of sex.

"Learn to be comfortable being uncomfortable."

Author: *Unknown*

Chapter 6

Side Door Philosophy

The Wisdom:

"Even after all this time, the Sun never says to the Earth, 'You owe me.' Look what happens with a love like that, it lights the whole sky." *~Hafiz*

The Event:

During Cali's soccer season, I spent three unsuccessful weeks trying to teach my daughter how to kick the ball with the top of her foot by the shoelaces and the side of her foot for better control. Back then, when she'd approach the other team's goalie, she would kick with toe point of her shoe and the ball would scream off in a direction she didn't intend. When coaching her, I thought I was doing everything right:

- I praised the correct kicking style
- I spoke in pictures she could clearly understand
- I was patient…most of the time
- And I absolutely believed in my girl

She did great in the living room and at the park, but when it came to the excitement of the game, she leaned back into kicking the ball with the toe point of her shoe. Yes, I was beyond frustrated. Then, something happened that surprised me. A father showed up to one of the games I had never seen before and stood next to me.

"What's the score?"

"We're up 3-1…I haven't see you before, I'm London."

"Nice, I'm Frank."

"Frank, which one's your daughter?"

"#12…yours?"

"#4."

"Wow, she's fast."

"Yeah."

And in that moment, it came to me.

"Frank, tell Cali to kick with her laces."

"What?"

"Tell her…to kick with her laces. Use her name when you do it."

He looked at me crazy.

"C'mon, Frank, it's for the team."

He turned and waited for Cali to get close to the ball in a tornado of girls.

"Cali, kick with your laces."

And she did. She kicked with her laces for the first time ever in a game and for the rest of the season. At least most of it.

The Action Item:

Decide that you will show and practice unconditional love with your daughter. Meaning, you will love her without conditions.

You will love her even when she doesn't listen to

you, internalize your advice, or kick the ball with her laces after you worked on it with her for three weeks straight, in the house, at the park, canceled important engagements, and then listens to some stranger-danger dude who she's never seen and suddenly does exactly what you've unsuccessfully tried to coach her to do.

Decide to be comfortable getting help, reaching, teaching, and guiding your daughter as she grows into a "Live Better" Daughter.

Decide to lasso your ego and not take actions to make your daughter feel guilt for finding or understanding an alternate way to become a "Live Better" Daughter.

Decide to be more aware of your event-based insecurities. That event at Cali's game momentarily made me feel like:

- My daughter didn't respect me
- She takes advice from strangers
- I wasted three weeks of my time
- I suck as coach
- My daughter doesn't trust me

I could go on but you get the point.

These feelings didn't last long, only until the end of the game. It was my ego that was bruised, not my character.

Decide today to laugh at your ego and to praise the fact that your daughter will learn, reach, stretch, and grow in many positive ways without you.

The Take Away:

My Grammy, my grandmother, used to say, "Baby, with that one right there, you're going to have to use the side door."

She was speaking about Cali and the fact that she and I are so alike. I've affectionately called it the Side Door Technique. When there is a lock on the front door of communication between you and your daughter, go through the side door:

- Her BFF (best friend forever)
- Her #2 BFF
- A coach she trusts
- Another parent she admires
- A teacher she adores
- A stranger-danger dad on the sidelines at her soccer game

Many times, when another voice says the exact same thing you have previously said, it strikes your daughter in a different way. And sometimes, a more effective and impactful way.

Decide to care more about the message getting through vs. being the messenger.

The Resource:

Book: *The Awakened Family* by Shefali Tsabary,

The Straight Whiskey, No Chaser:

Don't grandmothers and grandmother-type individuals give the best advice? Guess what, guys? We don't hear that advice if our mouth is moving or if we're focused on ourselves.

It's about the art of effective, deep, and intuitive listening. Not just hearing the words, not just hearing the vibration of the cilia in our ears, but really feeling where your daughter is coming from.

Our elders have so much wisdom. Get around them, the ones that are respectable, the ones that have books in their minds, and those that have 75+ years on this planet. I love libraries and when you look into the eyes of these individuals it's like you're walking through the doors of a library.

And the reality is, when they take their last breath that door will close forever. They are walking institutions of wisdom, tools with the ability to solve complex problems, and the source of our smiles and security.

They've been there, seen that, and done that. Some elders have people in their own family who won't listen to them. And here's where you and I

come in. Get around an elder. Gain some wisdom.
Gain some knowledge.

They may talk for two hours and you get 60
seconds worth of gold, however, that gold can last
a lifetime for you, your daughter, and for the love
you co-create together.

Chapter 7

Create Your Refresh Rate

The Wisdom:

"Absorb what is useful, discard what is not, add what is uniquely your own." ~*Bruce Lee*

The Event:

While making pancakes together, my daughter asked me, "Daddy...how'd you learn to be a good daddy?"
"By making lots of mistakes and trying lots of new things, babe."
She smiled and moved on.

"You want blueberries and strawberries or just blueberries this time?"
"Both of 'em, sweetie."

The Action Item:

Decide that you will add a Refresh Rate protocol to your routine concerning being your daughter's father.

I am in the gym or do some form of exercise 6 days a week. Every three weeks, I take one of those exercise days and spend that time researching new routines, interesting fitness people, new nutrition philosophies, and unique physical therapy exercises to protect my muscles, bones, and joints as I get younger, as I get younger, in case you didn't hear me...as I get younger.

Every three weeks, I absorb what is useful, throw away what's not working, and take time to think, discover, and challenge why I do what I do, very much like the spirit of the Bruce quote I shared.

I do the same with being a father, a protector, a guide, and her first love. Once every three weeks, I search for new information, philosophies, and interesting people who are experts on feminine self-esteem, positive body psychology, fun memory exercises, female assertiveness teachings, female entrepreneurs, womenomics, and more.

She motivates me to discover for her, share with her, and **be a constant resource for her.**

Decide how often you will refresh your thoughts, actions, and habits on how you perform as a world class dad in training. Every 3 weeks, 6 weeks, or 12 weeks? Whatever the length of time that works best for you...decide to create a Refresh Rate. If not for you, then do it for her.

Take Away:

When you create a Refresh Rate, you become a resource for her, and you cultivate a habit of your little girl, no matter her age, coming to you for answers, to be her soundboard, or to point her in the right direction.

Decide to frequently challenge the results of your actions and being her father. If what you are doing is real and beneficial, it will withstand any test.

Remember, truth welcomes any challenge.

Your actions and what you believe will not be offended by being tested. Truth doesn't take challenge personally, egos do.

Are you familiar with the popular belief that it takes 21 days to create or change a habit? The theory came from Maxwell Maltz and his book, *Psycho-Cybernetics, A New Way to Get More Living Out of Life*. Personally, I own the book and agree with many of its concepts.

However, I disagree with Maxwell's 21 days theory. Why? The book was published in 1960. Do you believe your environment has an impact on your habits? In 1960:

- The cell phone didn't exist
- World War II was still fresh in the world's collective consciousness
- JFK, Dr. Martin Luther King, and Marilyn Monroe were still alive
- The state of Mississippi still had "Colored" and "White" signs above some public drinking fountains
- There was no XBox 360, Netflix, IKEA, Tesla, and gas was .25/gallon

The context of time and environmental conditions was simply different. That's why I disagree with Maxwell's theory. It may have been relevant then but not as much now.

If you choose not to filter lemonade before you drink it, you may swallow a few seeds.

What does that mean? As times change, so, too, does context and wisdom, and you need to filter out the seeds.

Habits are created and sustained based on the individual and the strength of emotional circumstances. My grandmother smoked at least one pack of Camel unfiltered cigarettes a day for more than 20 years and one day, she quit cold turkey. Her reason? She wanted to see her grandson graduate high school. A strong emotional circumstance lead to the change of a 20 year addictive behavior in one second.

How long has it taken many politicians to develop the habit of being consistently honest or transparent? How long did it take Oprah Winfrey to achieve a body weight in which she felt comfortable in her beautiful brown skin? More than 21 days for both examples? Yes.

Decide to frequently test your beliefs of being her dad:
- Why do you do what you do?
- Does the context matter?

- How's your current approach working for you?
- How's your current approach working for her?

Challenge and improve your current actions of being her dad by adding a refresh rate that works for you.

Resource:

Book: *The Code of An Extraordinary Mind* by Vishen Lakhiani
Podcast: I love Marketing – Episode 254 – Vishen Lakhiani

The Straight Whiskey, No Chaser:

You know what the hardest thing about this refresh rate is? Making the time. Not taking the time but making the time. Whatever that means to you, putting it on the calendar, planning it, or scheduling it you have to make the time.

You have to develop an appetite to learn, master, teach, and learn again…learn, master, teach, and learn again.

Over time grow more positive habits, your confidence as a father, and grow a richer level of trust between you and your daughter.

"Absorb what is useful, discard what is not, add what is uniquely your own."

Author: *Bruce Lee*

Chapter 8

When Not to Be Sorry

The Wisdom:

"Every time you lie to yourself, you lose power to speak with conviction." Author: Unknown

The Event:

"Dad, take a look at..."
She noticed I was on my phone, left, and came back when I was off.
"Sorry, Dad, I didn't know you were on the phone."
"Why are you sorry?"
"Because you were on the phone."
"Was it an accident?"
"Of course..."
"Then you don't need to be sorry, babe."
"But I felt bad."
"Alright, listen close, mama. It's okay to feel bad for a moment. After that, put a clock on it and decide how long you will allow yourself to feel bad...it was an accident. Now, if you accidentally slammed the door on my hand, I could see you saying sorry for that. You accidentally hurt me. Interrupting a phone call doesn't hurt me. What is another word you could use besides sorry?"

The Action Item:

Decide you will listen to how your daughter uses "I'm sorry" or "I am sorry" even more closely than you have before. At the end of the conversation I just shared with you, we:

- Brainstormed words and phrases that conveyed how she really felt about the accident occurring instead of being 'sorry'
- Talked about what we both believed the word "context" meant
- Talked about the power of using the words "I am" and owning your power rather than giving it away

The Take Away:

When your daughter says sorry out of context, she:

- Assigns unnecessary blame to herself and damages her self-esteem
- Erodes the positive belief and intentions of her actions
- Deepens the pattern of feeling at fault for random accidents

Is this the type of mindset and reactionary behavior you desire your daughter to go through life with? Of course not.

My grandmother told me once, "Don't ask someone not to do something unless you give them something to replace it with."

Meaning, if you ask your daughter to not say 'sorry' as frequently, what can she say to fill the space while she develops the habit of saying sorry at the right time in the right context?

Again, put your thinking cap on. Experiment with different words that allow her to feel she's being polite and respectful in addition to not assuming she has done something wrong.

A few examples are:

- Pardon me/Excuse me
- That was close/Not so perfect timing, huh?

My daughter, Cali, uses "Pardon me" spoken with a French accent (Pard-own-mwoah) to add fun to and personify her new reactionary behavior. For her, the fun of adding a personality or character to the new habit helps enforce the right way to respond to simple accidents.

Here's an invitation to run your own experiment. Count the number of times in a day you hear any female say sorry vs. a male. Be your own resource. Conduct your own research. Develop your own opinion through experience.

The Resource:

Book: *The Power of I AM.* by Joel Osteen
Video: The Power of I AM. Dr. Wayne Dyer

The Straight Whiskey, No Chaser:

If you choose to accept this mission I can neither confirm nor deny the success of your results.

For those of you daring enough, when you do this experiment hit me up on Twitter @londonporter and let me know what your results are.

First, allow me to share some mathematics with you. If your daughter is 10 years old and she has been saying "I'm sorry" for the last five years, what percentage of her life is that?

50%. Now, take an adult. If they've been smoking for 10 years and they're 40 years old, what percentage of their life have they been engaged in that bad habit? 25%.

- In this example the adult has been performing the bad habit for more years than the child.

- The child has been performing the bad habit for more of her life than the adult.

Therefore, keep in mind how much time it will take to change a habit based on how long the habit has existed in your daughter's life.

Kids with braces have them on for years in most cases because it took years earn crooked teeth.

Straighten any crooked critical thinking and analytical skills you may have.

One more kinesthetic example. If you naturally wear you watch your left wrist:

- Put it on the opposite wrist and see how comfortable that feels.

- Notice how much extra time it takes,

- Did you get frustrated quickly?

- Did you feel clumsy, foolish, a little incompetent?

This is a quick, physical exercise to help you cool your results-oriented-jets when your daughter makes mistakes as she's cultivating the habit of changing "I'm sorry" to "I apologize" to "pardon me" or something else the two of you create together.

"Every time you lie to yourself, you lose power to speak with conviction."

Author: Unknown

Chapter 9

What Role Will Grades Play in Her Life?

The Wisdom:

"Grades don't measure intelligence and age doesn't define maturity." Author: Unknown

The Event:

"Hey, sweetness, London gave me his report card, did you get yours today?"
"Yes."
"Can I see it?"
"Don't be mad at me, okay?"
"Why would I be mad at you?"
"Because you got mad at London last time."

The Action Item:

Decide:

- How much power you will allow school grades to have in your daughter's life
- As best you can, objectively analyze how society has or has not conditioned you to think about education
- As we move into the robotics age of machine and man, occasionally revisit your belief on the role of traditional education in your daughter's life

Back to the conversation with Cali and I.

"Cal, what exactly did I get mad at London for?"

"His missing assignments."

"Do you think his missing assignments made his grades lower?"

"Yes."

"If you were London's dad, what would you have said about his grades?"

"To turn in his assignments next time."

"I agree with you. I was mad at London's effort, not his grades. I was mad at something London did not do, not who London is as a person. Babe, do you understand the difference?"

"I think so."

"Tell me what you think I said."

"What London does and him as a boy are different."

"Yes, now, let's look at how many missed assignments you had."

The Take Away:

Some time ago, one of my mentors asked me how my college degrees, that he knew I was so proud of at the time, was working out for me. He was really asking me about my bank account, my ability to teach others, my ability to create value for others, he was asking me how my education made me a better Renaissance Man. My Alpha Male Ego shriveled underneath the Las Vegas July sun rays of that question. From that day on, I saw education differently. Back to Cali...

"Dad, I don't have any missing assignments."

"Exactly, you know what that means?"

"You're not mad?"

"No, silly goose. You did your best."

"I really did. And I don't read as good as London."

"And I don't expect you to. London is a better reader and you're a better speaker and story teller."

"That's true."

"And…I got mad at London for his effort, not his…"

"Grades."

"Exactly."

"But you're not mad at me because I tried, right?"

"No, I'm not. Now, let's talk about what you're not understanding in the class you got the C in."

I wish I could tell you I've always been this way, that I didn't' screw up many, many, many times before, that I didn't previously feel guilty for mis-educating my daughter about what role grades should play in her life. But I can't. I didn't begin to change until I got mad enough at the asinine results I was getting at being a mediocre dad…and then started to question everything I knew.

But then again, had I not tripped over my own ego and lack of intelligence, you and I might not be talking with each other right now.

If my failures, growth, and success as a father helps one young girl growing into a woman believe in her father even 1% more...the time I invested in you, in me, in this audio...is worth it.

The Resource:

Ted Talk: Do Schools Kill Creativity? by Ken Robinson

Ted Talk: The Best Kindergarten You've Ever Seen, by Takaharu Tezu

The Straight Whiskey, No Chaser:

Many women in the survey put a high value on education. What they really meant was wealth creation, independence, and a woman that can provide for herself in today's capital market system.

This philosophy was different from the feminist approach of not depending on a man.

Back to the topic of grades. If you haven't already, you'll probably make this mental shift faster than I did. The shift of focusing on what grades do for your daughter rather than what grades she receives on a piece of paper.

For example, these days...when Cali comes home, the first place we look is in the column for missed assignments. We always start with the amount of effort she put into her school work and move on from there.

Then, I started to do some critical thinking and asked myself, "Okay, what is the end result? What do I want Cali's education to do for her?"

The end result was that I wanted my girl to be out there doing things in the world, helping people, solving problems, and earning phenomenal money.

 I wanted her to know she doesn't have to live paycheck to paycheck and she can actually take dad on a vacation or out for dinner and me not foot the bill. That's the end result.

It's not about the grade. It's about the ability to create and earn her keep in this world...on her own terms. And the ability comes from the habit of smart, consistent, and applied effort.

Then came the epiphany, **she needs to learn entrepreneur skills.** Even if she's going to work for an organization or a person, she needs to learn how to illustrate and believe in her value.

Joe Polish, Dean Jackson, Marie Forleo, Brendon Burchard, Sybil Chavez, Danielle LaPorte, Jeff Walker, Eben Pagan, are online entrepreneurs.

We need to teach our daughters entrepreneurial skills because it teaches her how to create value, solve problems in the world, make our planet better, and create revenue for herself on demand.

If that revenue changes to bit coin or some other type of integrated approach, the medium is not what's important…it's about solving problems and creating value in the marketplace. That's what's important.

Creating value is the education most school systems fail to teach. And that is your responsibility as a father, your responsibility as a dad, as a mentor, and as a man raising a young woman.

Live Better Dads create Live Better Daughters. Teach her or at least introduce her to the concept of developing entrepreneurial skills.

"Grades don't measure intelligence and age doesn't define maturity."

Author: Unknown

Chapter 10

Own Her Power or Give It Away

The Wisdom:

"He who angers you controls you."
Author: Unknown

The Event:

"How was your day, sweetie?"
"Brandon made me so mad."
"Oh, really…and…"
"He was being a little diva and trying to get attention while we were testing…it was so annoying."
"What did your teacher say?"
"He only did it when she wasn't looking or walked out of class for a minute."
"What exactly annoyed you?"
"I was trying to concentrate and he was just so distracting."
"What did he do when you told him he was being annoying?"
"I didn't. We were testing, you're not supposed to talk when testing."
"Is he supposed to be annoying and distracting during testing?"
"No."
"Do you think it is okay to break the rules in a good way if someone is breaking the rules in a bad way?"
"I guess."

"Humph...you're a smart girl...I'm sure you'll figure it out."

The Action Item:

When you see an opportunity to teach, share, or reinforce the habit of your daughter owning her own power, decide that you will act on it immediately, or as close to the event as possible.

Later that night, after Cali told me about the annoyance of her day, I asked, "Hey, babe, when you were talking about Brandon, did he make you upset?"
"He sure did."
"Does Brandon have a remote control that makes your body move?"

"No..."
"Is he a mind freak and jumps inside your head to make you think specific thoughts?"
She laughed, "No."
"Who has the control and power to make Cali upset or annoyed?"
"I do."

I didn't have to go much further. Cali understood that she's in control, she has the power, and other people don't control how she feels, not even me.

As with any teaching or lesson to be learned, your timing and your tone are crucial. You never want your daughter to feel:

- Embarrassed
- Ashamed
- Not safe around you
- Like you are passive aggressively saying, "I told you so," or "See what happens when you don't listen to me."

I've screwed this one up with my Lieutenant London tone so many times in the past. I am a continuous work in progress.

And I wish I could give you a perfect formula or blueprint with respect to tone and timing; however, that's not possible. The relationship between you and your daughter is unique, so is the tone and timing you co-create through your life-long interactions. Simply be more aware and experiment with tone and timing. Keep what works. Toss out what doesn't.

The Take Away:

What life goals or aspirations do you have for your Lil' Lady?

- College graduate?
- Successful in business?
- Be a famous athlete, model, or actress?
- Be happy?
- Fall in love with someone who honors and deserves her?

- Have healthy children?
- Find her major passion in her life?
- Stop asking you for money?

Do you believe if your daughter gets better at, or masters, owning her own power, she would make better future decisions about?

- Her academic education?
- How she treats and values her body?
- Being more aware of situations that could physically harm her?
- Her personal development?
- Her financial independence?
- Her romantic relationships?
- Her emotional stability and well-being?
- Her reactions to major and minor setbacks in life?

When your daughter understands how and why owning her power adds confidence, security, and a sense of certainty to her ever changing world…she will one day, in her own special way, thank you for being the man who shared this principle with her.

The Resource:

Book: *Emotional Intelligence 2.0* by Travis Bradberry and Jean Greaves
The Straight Whiskey, No Chaser:

Here's how the chapter "Own Her Power or Give it Away" shook loose from the tree branches of the survey. I heard women say things like:

Fathers really need to teach their daughters how to respect themselves, how to love herself, how to set boundaries in romantic relationships, in friendships, how to not be sorry all the time, and how to not think of themselves as bossy but think of themselves as having leadership skills. Like Sheryl Sandberg's book, Lean In, that's what fathers need to teach their daughters.

I took all of those ideas and wrapped them up in a bow that meant this: Teach her how to own her power not give it away. One of the challenges with raising a strong independent woman is, you're dealing with a strong independent woman.

"He who angers you
controls you."

Author: Unknown

Chapter 11

Be Her Imagination Idol

The Wisdom:

"Logic will get you from A to B, imagination will take you anywhere." ~Albert Einstein

The Event:

"Daddy, you're so crazy."
"You know what they say about crazy people, right?"
"What?"
"It's the people who say they aren't crazy you may want to watch more closely."
I started dancing around.
"You're the best dad ever…"
"Why is that, sweetness?"
"You see things other dads can't see."

The Action Item:

Decide that you will be a role model for how your daughter can use her imagination. And the wicked beautiful fact that you can tuck in your wallet is this…no matter what age your daughter is now, you're never to late to show her your imagination wheelhouse. Even if you don't feel like you have one, you can always make the choice to start developing one.

Disclaimer: Developing or openly showing imagination can be challenging for some men. I was one of them. I had to swallow my pride and ask for help. I found someone I believed was creative and demonstrated what my daughter and her close friends thought was creative and imaginative.

Remember, a closed mouth doesn't get fed. And if your current lack of confidence or machismo ego prevents you from asking, still find those people and observe. Watch and listen from a safe distance and study exactly what they do and say to be so fun to be around, to make people smile, and make them feel safe.

Imaginations tips and strategies:

When she's 10 and under:

- Make up silly bed time stories
- Read books together and take turns making up new endings
- Create fun daytime stories before or after school
- Call her on the phone from a planet far far away

When she's 11 to 17:

- Let her see you using your imagination for your work
- Research famous or popular people she fancies, discover specific ways in which her 'idols' use their imaginations, and share what you found with her

- Play games that allows both of you to laugh deep Buddha belly laughs together
- Read and share books with her that challenges her imagination to grow

When she's 18 and above:

- Ask her for advice on one of your visualization techniques. That's your cue to create one or some if you don't have any
- Ask her to show you how she uses her imagination
- Ask her to score you on a scale of 0-10, 10 being all the time and 0 being hardly ever, concerning how often she believes you use your imagination.
- Ask her if she believes imagination and visualization are important factors in her life? And how?

The Take Away:

When you champion your daughter's imagination, you allow her to develop the confidence and belief that whatever she dreams is possible. That skill will be by her side during unfavorable situations when you're not around to be her hero. What's that worth to you?

The Resource:

Ted Talk: How to Build Your Creative Confidence by David Kelley

The Straight Whiskey, No Chaser:

"My dad was so crazy. My dad was so cool. My dad was so fun. I was so lucky. He was just a great guy." Then, I also heard women say, "I wish my dad was funny. I wish my dad was that cool. I wish my dad didn't have an engineer mindset and wasn't so devoid of emotion."

You know what's interesting about the imagination? You don't have to be the one to have a great imagination, the funny guy, or the person who is fun to be around.

Really!

For example, go to YouTube.com and type in the first comedian that enters your mind. Start to listen, watch, and really observe what you find funny about that person. Chances are you have some of those same elements in you too.

All it takes is your deciding to develop a habit of being around funny people, situations, and scheduling time for activities that make you smile and laugh.

I guarantee you this. Some of the natural quirkiness, dry sense of humor, or naturally hilarious points about you will start to be expressed more often.

You'll know you're making progress when your daughter says different things like, "Dad, that was pretty good," or "Where'd that come from, that doesn't sound like you...but I like it."

The imagination is like a muscle. Use it or it will atrophy.

"Logic will get you from A to B, imagination will take you anywhere."

Author: Albert Einstein

Chapter 12

Show Her God

The Wisdom:

"I believe in the sun when it's dark, I believe in love when my heart cries, and I believe in God when I feel empty inside. I believe."
Author: Unknown

The Event:

"Dad, who's God?"
"Good question, Cal. Who do you think God is?"
"I don't think God is a man."
"Why is that?"
"Because men weren't always nice to women back then. And God is always nice."
"Then, is God a woman?"
"No, God is God. And God doesn't have to be a person."
"That's interesting, Cal, tell me more."
"Remember when you said something makes the sun come up every morning?"
"Yeah."
"And I don't have to think about my heart beating, it just does?"
"Yes."
"I think that's God...the one who makes all those things happen."
"You know what, Cal?
"What?"
"You're one smart cookie....just one thing..."
"Umm hmm."

"Remember, you are never alone. Just like you said, God does all those things…God is always with you and…inside you."

"Inside, too?"

"Yes, ma'am. You know when you get the goosebumps…?"

"That's God?"

"Just one of the many ways God lets you know you're never alone."

The Action Item:

Children are magnificently wise.

Decide today, how you will allow your daughter to discover God in her own way? Or give her your view of God and begin the path of telling your daughter how to take direction from a man before trusting her inner self, her inner voice of God.

The Take Away:

Has any part about this chapter triggered your emotion? Is your heart beating faster right now? Do you believe that man is superior to women?

Remember, this book is not advice. This book is a tool to question, discover, and refine your higher thinking. Not western thinking with your brain, thinking with your entire being. This book is about you and me being a Live Better Dad so we can raise Live Better Daughters.

If you agree with every thing that one person has said, chances are, you're not thinking for yourself.

Showing your daughter God will provide her strength in life on the days and moments you are not able to.

Whether God, Allah, Buddha, Source, Universe, Yahweh, Jehovah, or invite your daughter to know there is a positive force that keeps the trillions of universes neatly organized in the night sky just as it keeps the trillions of cells underneath her skin in harmony…what the two of you decide to call that force…is yours to discover.

The Resource:

Close your eyes, open your heart, take one deep breath, and ask for the resource to be shown to you.

The Straight Whiskey, No Chaser:

Gentlemen, reach out to me @londonporter on Twitter. If you have ideas, suggestions, interesting stories, wisdom, or if you have something to say concerning raising confident women, then let it be heard.

"Be ashamed to die until you have won some victory for humanity." Author: Horace Mann

"Listen to the whispers from your soul's heart...that my Love, is the way to God."

Author: Randall Emerson

About The Author

London Porter

A little bit about the author, this fella who's been conversing with you named London Porter. I often get the question, "Hey, is that your real name…London?"

My status quo reply, "Yes, that's what it says on my drivers license, social security card, and my birth certificate." However, I wasn't born with the name London. Here's how and why I became London in the year 2001.

If you're young enough, do you remember Y2K? Back in 1999, the news was all abuzz about apocalyptic times, society was doomed, and the world would soon be going to hell in a hand basket?

I had just moved from Austin to Dallas, Texas and was of the attitude, "If the world is going to hell, I'm going to hell in a party."

December 11, 1999 is when I first stepped foot on Vegas soil. When I arrived, I moved in with my best friend, Dominic. We spent New Year's Eve on the bridge in front of the Venetian Hotel and Casino. Two women sporting Angel's costumes shared my space and that was the best fireworks show I've ever seen in my life.

At the time, Dominic was a music producer doing the score for a movie directed by Kelly Schwartz. I found myself on the set moving wires, setting up scenes, and simply being helpful.

Kelly rolled up on me one day and said, "Hey, how comfortable are you wearing suits?"
I tell him, "I do that all day every day and twice on Sunday. Why?"
"Have you ever acted before?"
"No."
"Do you think you could play a bad guy because you know…you seem kinda' nice?"
"Kelly, I was in anger management class at 11 and 17. I think I can summon some old habits again."

He gave me the role and I played an FBI agent with a mean streak, running around, and killing people. Two months go by and the main actor's shots were complete.

Kelly says, "Hey, we're doing the credits, how do you want your name to read?"
"Just use my name."
He said, "No, how do you want your name to read?"

"Kel, put my name. Randy Porter."
He scoffed, "No, No, No. Listen, Tom Cruise, Cruise isn't his real last name. Nicholas Cage, Cage isn't his real last name."

Then, I realized something that changed my life forever.

I could be anybody I wanted to be. With conviction I said, "London Porter."

"Oh, that sounds strong. Where'd that come from?"

"I don't know but I like it. London Porter."

Kelly said, "All right."

Fast forward two more months, we're on Las Vegas Blvd debuting the movie, Kelly walks to me and says, "Hey, Randy."

"Uh, no. It's London."

"Oh, that's right...London" as he heckled me while positioning his fingers in quotation marks.

I took my wallet out, put it in his chest, and he started looking through it.

"Social security card, credit cards, drivers license, school ID...oh my God...you are crazy."

"No, I'm London." We both laughed and had a great rest of the night.

That was back in my mid-20's. And guys, I'm slightly embarrassed to tell you, **that was the first time in my life that I believed I could be whatever and whoever I wanted to be.** And that is how London Porter was born.

Twitter @LondonPorter
www.LondonPorter.Co
www.iblb23.com

Live Better Dads
Live Better Daughters

LBD

11 Power Principles,
Conscious Dads,
Real Results

Also in: *Audio Format*

BY: LONDON PORTER